MW00817555

IMAGES
*of America*

# LOWVILLE

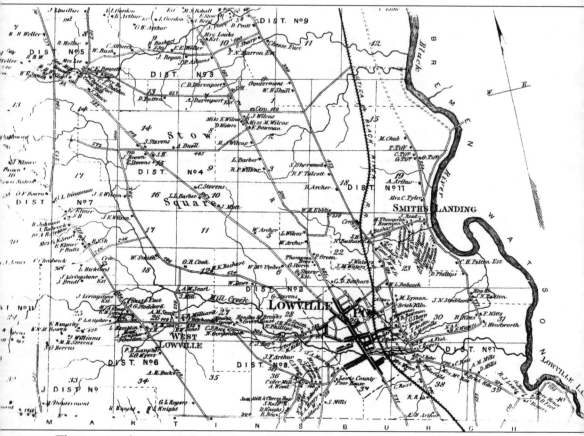

This image is from an 1875 atlas of Lewis County and shows Lowville and the surrounding area as it appeared during that period, with the Black River Landing sites and streets. (Thomas R. Duflo collection.)

*On the cover*: Please see page 101. (Thomas R. Duflo collection.)

IMAGES
*of America*

# LOWVILLE

Dorothy K. Duflo
Foreword by Charlotte M. Beagle

ARCADIA
PUBLISHING

Copyright © 2009 by Dorothy K. Duflo
ISBN 978-1-5316-4259-4

Published by Arcadia Publishing
Charleston, South Carolina

Library of Congress Catalog Control Number: 2008942674

For all general information contact Arcadia Publishing at:
Telephone 843-853-2070
Fax 843-853-0044
E-mail sales@arcadiapublishing.com
For customer service and orders:
Toll-Free 1-888-313-2665

Visit us on the Internet at www.arcadiapublishing.com

*To Tom, my sounding board, pillar, and taskmaster,*
*thanks for always being there.*

# CONTENTS

# ACKNOWLEDGMENTS

Going back to the beginning of Lowville's history enables one to view the course its first settlers took when they laid out a footprint with deliberate plans and foresight of what was to be. Guardians of this magnificent history are to be commended for their dedication in preserving it for future generations, such as Lewis County's first historian, Dr. Franklin B. Hough; town historian Charlotte M. Beagle; Lewis County Historical Association director and county historian Lisa Becker; Gordon Allen and other former editors of the *Lowville Journal and Republican*; Northern New York Library, which offers a wonderful service of vintage newspapers online; Judy Adams and Dawn Myers of Lowville Free Library; and Douglas P. Hanno, county clerk and "keeper of the courthouse records." Special thanks go to Michael K. Brown, Carol L. Moshier, and Carolyn Virkler for sharing their photographs; Darin Zehr, Patricia Burke, and Bonnie Virkler for their generous contributions; and Arcadia Publishing for presenting such an avenue to make this possible. Thanks to Shay E. P. Richards, Wildroot Bookstore, and Wayseeker Studios for getting the ball rolling. Unless otherwise noted, all images are from the collection of Thomas R. Duflo.

# FOREWORD

Some say that the only new history is the history that we do not know. Dorothy K. Duflo corrected that situation by providing a great deal of history known only to a few local historians. Now everyone who reads this vivid history will have the same access as the historians. This vibrant history of a Black River village demonstrates the national trends and issues that impact local areas. While land speculator Nicholas Low named Lowville, it was not a formal village until 1854. A year after the formal incorporation of Lowville, the population reached 908; the 2000 U.S. Census counted 3,476 individuals. This edition illustrates the institutions that shaped the inhabitants of Lowville and consequently the nation.

This new history of Lowville includes the best of an eclectic collection of images. Each image has a caption that identifies the location and people as they react to their present. My favorites are the postcards of the first run of legal alcoholic beverages after the 21st Amendment to the U.S. Constitution repealed the 18th Amendment. One wonders if the image of a bottle in the hand was legal booze or not.

The milk strike of the 1930s reminds one that New Yorkers considered this rural revolt to be the result of agitation by communists. Edmund Wilson, a renowned 20th-century author with Lewis County antecedents, vouched that the farmers "were indignant at being called communists." Duflo's photographs of agriculture illustrate its impact on Lowville's businesses. The Lowville Post Office was a project of the Public Works Administration that provided jobs during the Great Depression. Duflo's photographs link the local to the national. A few photographs, rarely seen except by the fire department, demonstrate the importance of volunteer firemen in preserving their response to fires that threatened the homes and businesses of the village.

This collection of images adds to the histories of Dr. Franklin B. Hough and G. Byron Bowen, which included the story of Lowville from the first settlers to the 1970s. They provide the essence of the story from Macomb's Purchase in 1791 to the 1970s. Duflo provides powerful images that validate the history of one small village in the north country. Her captions provide significant detail to interest both the historian and those who are curious about the past.

Charlotte M. Beagle
Constable Hall Association executive director
Town of Lowville historian

7

# INTRODUCTION

Lewis County was once a part of Macomb's Purchase, formed from Oneida County on March 28, 1805. It received its name from Gov. Morgan Lewis. The area lies principally within the Black River valley and the layout, which is generally low and inclines toward the Black River on both sides. Nicholas Low, a principal investor from New York City, drew township number 11—later known as Lowville—in a lottery for the Black River Tract, with Silas Stow appointed as his agent.

Stow purchased a tract in the center section of the area and set aside a large parcel for the Presbyterian church in the northwest corner known as Stow Square. The event took place on April 20, 1798, the same date the first deed was issued to Daniel Kelley. Kelley built a sawmill on the south side of Mill Creek just below the bridge, and the following year, a gristmill was raised with the aid of settlers from around the county. Kelley's mills, an inn built by Capt. Jonathan Rogers, and Fortunatus Eager's store determined the location of the village, as it was developed mostly on the Rogers farm.

The village was incorporated in 1849, and a charter was adopted in 1854. A village water system was implemented in 1894, with the construction of a 17-mile pipeline from a spring-fed two-million-gallon reservoir erected on acquired lands in Watson. Water was turned into village mains in 1895 when a schedule of water rates was adopted. Private meters were sold under the control of an established water board. Hotels were the first to receive electricity in 1887, streetlights were turned on the following year, and the sewage treatment plant was built in 1938.

During a period of industrial growth in 1903, leading businessmen felt the need to form a corporation that could be used to build and operate a railroad, which would help the region to grow and expand outside its boundaries. Out of this came the Lowville and Beaver River Railroad, which became one of the leading transportation devices for the many products that were grown or produced in the area. One such product was from Fulton Machine and Vise Company on Trinity Avenue. In 1917, with 65 employees, it produced 100 vises a day for contracts with the American and French governments. The firm developed financial problems after the end of World War I and was sold at auction in 1930.

In 1876, brothers John E. and George J. Haberer bought a furniture factory on Valley Street and relocated the plant to Trinity Avenue east of the railroad line. John took over the factory, and George was in charge of the retail side of the business and undertaking. John's son Northam later managed the factory of 100 employees, with furniture shipped primarily to New York City and Philadelphia. When the South began to emerge as the new manufacturing center, he closed the doors by 1931.

Harold A. Payne and James Jones started a business in New Jersey in 1932 under the name of Payne and Jones and then moved to Lowville. They bought the old Beaverland Corporation building on Bostwick Street, and, with the trade name of Pajco, the company manufactured rolls of material used primarily for checkbooks and catalogs. The business expanded in 1956, purchasing the old foundry property in back that was once part of Haberer Furniture on Trinity Avenue, and is currently Fibermark North America, Inc.

In 1957, the United Block Company, a subsidiary of American Machine and Foundry, bought the property owned by the ABC Company on Trinity Avenue to finish bowling pins. In 1960, the company purchased the American Seating Company plant near the southern limits of the village. It is now known as Quibica AMF, the sole manufacturer of U.S. bowling pins. It also manufactures 95 percent of the world's supply. Earlier wood lanes are now synthetic and are mainly manufactured by AMF's plant in Virginia. Lowville's plant of 110 employees supplies 9,000 pins per day.

Climax Manufacturing was founded in Castorland in 1902 by Samuel Hirschey, who patented and produced the first chicken incubators in 1904. Eventually the company began producing cheese drums for dairy producers and boxes for florists and purchased a Carthage paperboard mill in 1939 to secure a reliable source of material. The plant, with five patents to its credit, relocated to Lowville in the mid-1980s and was sold by the Hirschey family in 2008. Liz Hirschey remains president of the plant, which has 262 full-time employees.

Lowville has been pivotal in the dairy industry since 1833 when Levi Bowen took the first load of cheese to Deerfield. In 1873, census reports for that period show cheese factories produced about eight million pounds of cheese annually with a value of $1 million. Now one of the largest milk sheds in the Northeast responsible for the biggest milk production in New York, it processes 65 percent of the milk made in the county.

Lowville Milk and Cream Company, east of the village on Bostwick Street, was built by father and son Brayton B. and Leon S. Miller in 1900, with Rufus J. Richardson later added as a partner. It was said to be the largest cheese cold-storage facility in the world with a maximum storage capacity of seven million pounds. Cheese shipped there was paraffined and reshipped all over the United States or held for future use. In 1928, it became the Lowville Cold Storage Corporation, a subsidiary of Kraft Phenix Cheese Company. Now known as Kraft Foods, it has 300 employees, is the biggest producer of Philadelphia Cream Cheese in the world, and processed more than 300 million pounds of milk in 2006.

Lowville Producers Dairy Co-Operative ranked 39th out of the country's top 50 cooperatives for production in 2007. It is noted that 78 percent of the milk in the United States was marketed by these top 50 cooperatives. Located on Utica Boulevard, it is owned by over 200 dairy farm families and has been in business since 1936. Its members produced 36 million gallons of grade A milk in 2008, with a value of $62.5 million before processing. The cheese outlet store features over 65 varieties along with many "Made in Lewis County" products.

Much is owed to Dr. Franklin B. Hough for his care in learning about the early businessmen and merchants who shaped Lowville's destiny and preserving the history of early settlements in Lewis County. The prestige noted earlier has been maintained, with Lowville still being the largest village in the county and one of the most desirable places in northern New York. The spirit lives on and prospers.

# One

# BYWAYS AND BRIDGES

One of the first roads constructed after the village was settled was Route 26 south through the "Eleven Mile Woods," as it was known then. It enabled settlers to take wheat to the gristmills in Turin and Whitestown. This 1914 image is just before the Mac Parks farm.

This image shows the village in the early 1900s, with Number Three Road just above the tree line to the left, Route 26 next the Methodist church steeple, and the fairgrounds on Jackson Street to the right center of the image.

This 1910 view of Lowville is from the Number Three Road looking southwest toward Rural Cemetery. The road was originally constructed to open travel to Township Three, or Rutland, and has been called this ever since. The large complex in the far distance is the county home on Stow Street.

NORTH END OF STATE ST. LOWVILLE. N.Y.
MANDEVILLE PHOTO.

Residential homes line the hill of Route 26 north of the village above Stewart Street in this 1910 photograph. The residence of Rev. Sanger B. Dewey, M.E., retired, is in view on the left side of the dirt road, and the sidewalk is a boardwalk.

BEECHES BRIDGE. NEAR LOWVILLE. N.Y.
PHOTO BY T.A.S. MILLER.

Beaches Bridge, which crosses the Black River into Watson, is seen in this early-1900s photograph by T. A. S. Miller. The area, called Smith's Landing, was the original site for settlers traveling up the Black River into Lowville.

13

In 1884, the High Bridge on Route 12 west of Lowville was built to cross Mill Creek, as seen in this 1907 view looking southeast. The wooden deck was narrow, however, and carriages coming from the opposite direction had to wait their turn before crossing the span.

On the State Road, Lowville, N. Y.

The second High Bridge widened the structure to two-lane traffic, making travel much easier. This 1910 view looks east, showing Route 12 and Clinton Street with a dirt surface. The Genevieve Strife house and barn can be seen on the hill after being relocated from the right side of the road during construction.

Construction on the new High Bridge began in November 1911, and this image shows what an immense project it was. Cement was poured all winter long except on the very coldest of days. The Town of Lowville did the construction, and the project was completed in early July 1912. (Gordon Allen collection.)

The highway department did such a good job that the bridge lasted until it was replaced professionally by Ballard Construction Company of Syracuse in 1974. At that time, around 73,500 cubic yards of dirt fill was brought in, the area was graded, and five steel girders were set in place before cement was poured. Ralph Martin of the state office building in Watertown was the project engineer.

*Working on state road near Lowville N.Y.*

Farmers customarily took care of the roads before there were highway departments, but in 1910, Walter R. Galloway, an engineer with the State of New York, was sent to Lewis County when the first section of macadam road was laid—a three-mile stretch from Lowville to the top of the hill at Martinsburg. (Judy Adams collection.)

*Working on State road in school house cut near Lowville N.Y.*

The road crew working on Route 26 encountered many obstacles in preparing the surface for paving. Large stone areas had to be cleared, and forms had to be placed before the work was completed. (Judy Adams collection.)

Village streets were paved in October 1912, with Warren Brothers of Boston, Massachusetts, awarded the contract. The old cobblestone pavement, which had been down for many years, was torn up, and the proper grade was made with bitulithic pavement used. E. A. Young of Boston was in charge of the crew. (Above, Gordon Allen collection.)

Working on pavement Lowville, N.Y. Oct. 17 1912

# Two

# SHOPS AND BUSINESSES

This early image of L. E. Bellinger Millinery Novelties looks south on State Street toward the Mill Creek bridge. On the left just past the bridge are Nortz's Cash and Carry and the Mammoth Building, also known as the A. N. Virkler Block, which is the current location of the parking lot for G. A. Nortz.

The section of State Street seen here in 1918 shows the Smiley and Times Buildings, which contained businesses, including (from left to right) Kotary's Meet Market, Grimm Market, Agens Jeweler, Davis Barbers, Jones and Goutremout Market, Tardy Jewelry, C. H. Ryan Candy, and Jacques Brothers. It is now the current location for (from left to right) Community Bank, N.Y. Pizzeria, Good Morning Realty, Wildroot Bookstore, Wayseeker Studio, Gallery 812, and the Dollar General (formerly the IGA).

The Black River National Bank, organized in 1879 and liquidated into the Lewis County Trust Company in 1920, was located on the corner of State Street and Shady Avenue. Other businesses housed there were Morgan and Stoddard Hardware, Farney's Soda Bar and Variety Store, and before 1880, the Lanpher House. The building was bought in 1964 by Lawrence Purvines and his sons, who operated an appliance store.

The photograph shown above was taken by William Mandeville on February 2, 1914, at the grand opening of the new Bijou theater. It later was renamed the Avalon and used until 1948 when it was destroyed by fire. Except for Donald Morse's Rambler and used car lot in the 1960s, the site was vacant until 1985 when Edgar S. K. Merrell II built the new law offices of Merrell and Merrell. (Carol Moshier collection.)

The brick building shown in this 1910 William Mandeville photograph was built in 1907 by G. S. Reed and housed the Lewis County Democrat (1867–1906), right, and the Electric Printing Company. Offices later included Duke Mihalyi Insurance and the law offices of George Reed, followed by Kenneth Wolfe. On the left, the small home is now Dimensions hair salon. The building on the corner of State Street and Trinity Avenue was built in 1909 by G. A. Blackmon and was later sold to the Virkler Funeral Home.

An early-1900s view of the busy corner at State and Dayan Streets shows Stoddard and Bateman, a dry goods store that occupied the site for many years, and H. F. Weber, Real Estate and Insurance, located upstairs. Continuing to the left are the Bostwick Clothing Store and the Fowler and Green Hardware store, which later became Cataldo Hardware.

The town hall was an opera house, as seen here in 1908. After the Avalon fire in 1948, it was completely remodeled, and moving pictures were again shown here. During World War II, the lobby was used as a United Service Organizations (USO) center. The corner of the building to the right was part of the Kellogg Block that was erected in 1885 and now houses Gary's Restaurant.

This 1910 image shows the delivery wagon for the Lewis Clothing House. The store offered a complete line of gentlemen's clothing and furnishings and was located in the block near the Central Hotel until 1941. The home to the right is located on the corner of Park and Shady Avenues and is now the offices for St. Peter's Church.

The Hiram Gowdy Quarry, shown in 1911, was located near the corner of Church and Water Streets. Located to the right of the building at the top of the hill is the old St. Peter's Church steeple, which was on the corner of Church Street and Highland Avenue until 1929 when the new parish was built and dedicated.

The lower business section of Dayan Street is shown in this early-1900s image. At back left is the new Howard C. Bingham building, which contained Bingham's monument business and a second store that was used by the Rufus J. Richardson Cheese and Produce company. Across the street is the fire department and village police office. The Lowville Men's Club had the Club House constructed on the south side of Dayan Street where the Dayan Street Opera House was once located. E. J. Smith bid on the job for $5,850, erecting the structure next to the Bingham building. The club was considered one of the most up-to-date club homes in northern New York. (Above, Lowville Free Library Collection.)

In 1882, Jacob Strife purchased Campbell's Hotel, located on the southwest corner of State and Stow Streets. It was enlarged by a two-story addition that served as a dining room and kitchen, and it was renamed the Strife House with a first-class stable attached in the rear. It was sold in 1920 to Henry and Adelaide Thisse where it was then renamed Henry's Hotel. Other owners included Frank Magra, Francis and Raphella Henry, and the final owner was Henry's son Albert in 1965. It was later sold and razed for the present business, Stewart's. The photograph below shows the Strife House on Stow Street with the Peter McGovern Carriage Shop in the center on the south side. The large barn to the right is the hotel livery stable and is currently Houpperts Creekside Furniture and Main's Antiques (left).

The Doig Block, as it appeared in this George Shepard image, was a very commercial area. Some of its larger shops were Brahmer's Clothing and Snyders Drug Store. Charles K. Doig entered into partnership with his brother Frank C. Doig in 1876, and the firm, known as Doig Brothers, was located on the corner of State Street and Shady Avenue. Jreck Subs, Cafe Z, W. B. Payne, and Sweet Basil are located there now.

Gerald C. Smith, chief of police, stands in the doorway of a local business in 1937. Also working for the village police at that time were Beryl Ide, special police, and Arthur Lyng, night watch. Duke, as he was more commonly referred to, served the village for an annual salary of $1,192.27. It is unknown how long he served in this position. (Patricia Burke collection.)

The lower end of the central business district can be seen in the 1907 view above of State Street, with the European Hotel, left, which occupied the upper floor of the two-story wooden structure. Window signage shows "Cigars" and "Café," left of the arched sign, and grocer B. L. Schermerhorn. Other businesses include Kellogg's Dry Goods, V. L. Waters, Kesler and Elliott, and Graham and Gasser. The hotel is on the corner of Exchange and State Streets, and the sign on the corner of the building advertises the Wideman and Robinson Livery Stable. The location is now Baker's Grill. The lower photograph, dated August 1907, shows a horse-drawn wagon in front of the Robinson livery with a uniformed driver aboard and a kitten underneath. (Below, Gordon Allen collection.)

This early view of the Lewis County Trust Company building was taken by photographer Henry M. Beach after the former Smiley Building was razed in 1921. Located around the corner is the Lowville Fire Department, and beyond is the Dayan Street Garage of Ira Gallup, who was killed during an explosion while repairing a gas truck on March 6, 1919. The building was sold to the village in 1947. (Carolyn Virkler collection.)

The Lewis County Home, a place that housed and fed the poor and elderly, was located on outer Stow Street and dates back to 1846. It also served as an insane asylum after 1884 for six years until the State Care Act required that the patients be moved to state-run facilities. Since the home grew a lot of its own food, guests could spend their days working on the farm or gardens of the estate.

The Virkler business was located on the southeast corner of State and River Streets. Owned by the Virkler family since 1887, it was purchased by Arthur N. Virkler from his father in 1916 and used to store cars for the first Ford agency in the village. In 1947, Franklin O'Hara purchased the block that also housed Farney's Buick. Farney's was located on the right, and O'Hara's Sport Shop and Kotary's Meat Market were on the left with the upstairs used for storage space. Gasoline was later offered at a pump conveniently located near the edge of the road. One of the two men clearing snow from the area is believed to be Ferd Duflo, who worked for Virkler and helped assemble the Model As when they arrived.

This 1907 image shows a glimpse of the village looking north down the hill into the lower end at State and Campbell Streets. The large building to the right is the Mammoth Block, which was Virkler's Ford Sales and Service, and the Bateman towers can be seen in the distance. The porch of the Strife House is left of the horse and carriage. In partial view near the top of the hill to the right of the white house with shutters is now the Gerald A. Nortz Chrysler-Dodge dealership.

The above view shows an ice delivery wagon pictured on the west side of State Street just outside the Marble and Granite Works and the Frank J. Bintz Restaurant and Saloon (right). The area is near Mill Creek bridge and where A Plus is now located. (Gordon Allen collection.)

The big cheese was made in Lewis County for the New York agricultural booth at the Panama-Pacific International Exposition in San Francisco in 1915. According to newspaper reports from the time, it weighed 15,000 pounds, required 150,000 pounds of milk to make, was four and a half feet high, and was close to seven feet in diameter. The cheese is shown in a specially made wooden crate and was on its way to the rail depot for shipping when photographed in front of the Bateman Hotel by William Mandeville. (Gordon Allen collection.)

Herbert D. Fairchild owned the meat market shown in this 1906 photograph, which was next to the *Lowville Journal and Republican* office on the east side of State Street. The open doorway, left, is the entrance to the Masonic Club located on the third floor of the building. The front of the store has quarters of fresh meat, such as beef and pork, and fresh-plucked chickens hanging outside. H and R Block is currently located in the building.

STRAWRIDE GIVEN BY H.D.FAIRCHILD.
ON LINCOLN'S BIRTHDAY. 1915. LOWVILLE, N.Y.
WEIGHT OF OXEN 4320 POUNDS

Herbert D. Fairchild ran the meat market from 1906 to 1918 and was quite active in the community. This 1915 William Mandeville photograph shows a straw ride, given by Fairchild to honor Abraham Lincoln's birthday, in a sled being pulled by a team of oxen that totalled a combined weight of 4,320 pounds. The location, which formerly housed the *Lowville Journal and Republican* newspaper, is presently owned by Roger and Britt Abbey and houses Dumbells Gym.

Another photograph of the same location with the name William Singer over the door was taken after 1918 when ownership passed on to him. Singer had worked as a butcher in the Fairchild business. Shown hanging are six large bucks that were brought in to be butchered and processed.

THE **BOSTWICK HOUSE**. LOWVILLE, N.Y.
ABOUT 1860 - 50 YEARS AGO.
WHERE NOW STANDS
THE BATEMAN.

The current building, known as the Bateman, was built on the footprint of the Bostwick House, a three-story steel-framed building that is shown here around 1860. Sometime in 1869, it was destroyed by fire and rebuilt by William Howell. Known as the Howell House, it had 108 feet of frontage and was four stories high. The two adjoining blocks were built at the same time with the same design, giving the appearance of wings to the central building. (Above, Carol Moshier collection.)

Howell House, Lowville, N. Y.
S. B. SAHLER, - - - - Proprietor.
(OVER.)

DOWN BY THE BROOK SIDE.
COPYRIGHTED, GUFFORD, BOSTON.

# KELLOGG HOUSE,

LOWVILLE, N. Y.,
## K. COLLINS KELLOGG,
*Owner and Proprietor.*

*SAMPLE ROOM FOR AGENTS.*

JOURNAL & REPUBLICAN STEAM PRINT, LOWVILLE.

K. Collins Kellogg owned this establishment in 1877, and the name was changed to the Kellogg House. The business offered a public café to the left of the main entrance and a sample room for agents to display their wares. It is noted that a mule-drawn wagon met every train to bring the salesmen and sample cases to the hotel.

Carroll H. Bateman was the proprietor in 1910, and the name changed to the Bateman. Extensive repairs followed, including the addition of a porte cochere over the sidewalk to the main entrance. It is presently owned by Conifer Realty, with the upstairs floors renovated into apartments. Roggies Flooring is located in the main entrance area, and A. A. and J. Insurance and Jennifer Meny Therapeutic Massage are in the remaining ground-floor office space. (Right, Carol Moshier collection.)

35

The main lobby of the Bateman, with its sweeping staircase, marble floor, elaborate tin ceiling, and open cigar boxes in the display case, is shown in this early view. The salesmen's sample room is shown with an open doorway to the right and chairs in the lobby to wait for customer appointments. The photograph below, dating from 1913, shows the Bateman bar with its very ornate woodwork and a spittoon on the floor. (Gordon Allen collection.)

Before the automobile was the main form of transportation, people traveled by railroad and stayed at area hotels. The hotels offered transportation to and from the hotels and met every train that came into the depot on Shady Avenue. During the summer, an open coach was used, as shown in the image of the Hotel Windsor vehicle (above), and in the winter months, a covered sled from the Kellogg House (below) was used.

The Central Hotel was located below the Bateman on the east side of State Street. Originally built during the Civil War, it had a lengthy history and many names on the deed. Some former owners included Daniel Doyle, the Kieb brothers, David Sheridan, William Elliott, John Duflo, Russell and Mary Duflo, Joseph Back, and William Singer. It was sold in 1964 to the Village of Lowville and razed to make way for a parking site. The land is now a driveway into the village parking area. (Gordon Allen collection.)

Hotel Windsor was located on the corner of State and Elm Streets and built in the mid-1880s by Robert N. Barr. Eleanor and Arel J. Brown had their wedding dinner there in 1945 when it was owned by Henry Twitchell, who noted it to be a great place for Sunday dinners. Taken over by Paul F. Hanno in 1956 and later by his brother David, it was torn down in the 1980s and combined with land from an adjoining property for what is now the location of HSBC Bank.

STATE ST. LOWVILLE, N.Y.

This 1907 image shows a large three-story brick building just south of the Central Hotel where the Asa C. Bellinger Barber Shop was located down a flight of stairs in the basement. Other businesses on the ground floor included a furniture store and undertaking business owned by the Fitch brothers, Lewis Clothing Company, and the Dorrance Bush meat market and grocery. The building was lost in a 1980s fire, and the property was later used for the Commons development. (Below, Gordon Allen collection.)

Noah Yousey worked in the woods of Wisconsin to earn money for an apprenticeship under blacksmith Peter McGovern, who operated a wagon shop on Stow Street. When his two-year training was completed in 1907, Noah bought a shop. His son Earl later joined in the trade, and as automobiles replaced horses, they began repairing them with Earl doing all the welding. The father and son team also invented a type of log bunker for trucks during the log boom. When Noah later became ill and retired, Earl ran the shop alone until it was decided to sell the building. He then moved the equipment to his home in West Martinsburg and worked for several more years. The photograph below shows Noah (left) and his brother Christian working on two horses in the shop. (Carolyn Virkler collection.)

The Lowville Farmer's Co-operative was incorporated in 1920, and at the same time, it purchased the Eugene Arthur Grain and Coal Company, with William B. Dening as general manager. A county-wide warehouse contract was made with the newly formed Grange League Federation, which required the cooperative to service all of Lewis County, enabling it to become the largest supply cooperative in the state. The demands of the county grew so large in the late 1930s that an agreement was made with the Grange League Federation to allow subdivisions and other cooperatives with the approval of the Lowville one. The men in the photograph below from left to right are Daniel Dening; William B. Dening, who retired in 1941; Claude McNeil; and Charles Liscum. Currently there are over 600 members, and John Williams of Carthage is president of the board of directors. (Above, Gordon Allen collection; below, Carolyn Virkler collection.)

Ver's Restaurant and Grill, owned by Louis VerSchneider, was located on the north side of Shady Avenue in the 1950s and boasted a bar and cocktail lounge separate from the dining area. The two-story structure was built in 1925 by Leon S. Miller. Miller had a small office on the second floor that was used for the Bryton B. Miller and Son cheese merchants. The post office was on the ground floor until a new one was built in 1939. Another space housed a few smaller businesses, one of which was the Duflo Restaurant, shown in the photograph below in 1930. It was operated by John C. Duflo until 1933 when he bought the Central Hotel. Jeb's Restaurant now occupies the west side of this site, with Black River Bakery and Corner Sun Hair Salon to the east.

Construction on the Lewis County Courthouse began in 1852 and was completed in 1855. It was constructed of brick at a cost of less than $6,000 and was used as a town hall until 1864 when the county seat was moved from Martinsburg. The clerk's annex (left) was added about 1900 when expansion was necessary. A devastating fire swept through the courthouse in 1947, destroying many valuable records, including half of the law library. When repairs were completed, the two sections of the building were connected. The Lewis County Jail and Sheriff's Office, shown in a 1917 photograph, was located on the east side of State Street between Water and Elm Streets. It was remodeled and updated in 1931 when, at that time, it had 12 cells and was separated by a firewall from the sheriff's quarters. (Below, Gordon Allen collection.)

LEWIS COUNTY JAIL AND SHERIFF'S OFFICE, Lowville, N. Y.

With automobiles more affordable and travel a necessity either for leisure or work, gasoline stations began to dot the horizon both in the village and outside. The photograph at left shows a uniformed service station operator pumping gasoline at a pump that is now Mullins Service Station. At this time in 1937, it is believed to have been owned by Alvin Kirch or Curtis and Kirch with the two homes on State Street still there today. The photograph below shows a gasoline station operated by May and Henry McKee on Dayan Street that is now Ed Yancey Sales and Service. (Left, Patricia Burke collection; below, Carol Moshier collection.)

This is an early-1900s image of the former F. L. Keegan Hotel, later purchased by the Lowville Farmers Co-operative and now their feed mill business. Looking north, the railroad depot is visible in the background on Shady Avenue. (Lowville Free Library Collection.)

TRINITY AVE. LOWVILLE, N.Y.

The residence of DeWitt C. West (left), located on the north side of Trinity Avenue, was later acquired by Lowville Academy and razed for the tennis courts. Horace Bush owned the house now occupied as the Butterscotch House Bed and Breakfast.

Contractor Sam Plato began construction on the new Lowville Post Office with the cellar excavated on August 1, 1939. The building was estimated at a cost of $100,000 and located south of the Dekin Building. The public tennis courts can be seen at the top left of this photograph along with the back of some of the homes on Waters Terrace. Parkway Drive is not yet constructed. The area is now the location of Parkway Liquors, Dry Cleaning, Laundromat and Get It and Go diner. The white building at top right is now the Lowville Professional Building and Central New York Developmental Services Office.

The above photograph from October 1, 1939, shows a crew working on the foundation, removing forms after the concrete floor was cured. The view looks east across State Street with the Virkler Funeral Home at left, the present location of Hair Vogue, Dorothy Monnat Framing, and Foy Insurance. The large home at right was that of Dorothy Moran and H. M. Donohue, who sold to the Grand Union Supermarket, which became a parking lot. It was later purchased by the National Bank of Northern New York, and a building was erected there that is now Key Bank. The photograph below, taken in December 1939, shows walls and a loading dock completed. Lowville Academy and Central School can be seen to the left side of the new building.

The new post office was dedicated on June 22, 1940. The Sons of Veterans, Boy Scouts, and American Legion retired the colors with Milton Russum as bugler. The Lowville Academy band gave a concert, and Mrs. Raymond S. Richardson sang "God Bless America." Joseph Betterley of the post office headquarters in Washington, D.C., was the guest speaker. Katherine Nortz, postmaster, was chairperson of arrangements and later entertained official visitors at her home.

Lewis County General Hospital was designed by A. F. Gilbert of New York City and was built in 1931 by C. Deline and Company of Watertown on the former Easton estate on the west side of State Street. The village board was very instrumental and agreed to furnish water, a hydrant, and sewage and contributed $2,500 toward the purchase price if the project was completed within or adjacent to the village limits. (Gordon Allen collection.)

The Lowville Free Library was built in 1927 after Clara J. Reeder and Cora May Gould, daughters of the late Rufus J. Richardson, presented the library association with a site on Dayan Street in memory of their father. The Daughters of the American Revolution raised over $5,000, and a building fund of $7,000 was added to an ambitious drive to see the project completed. The library still depends on the generosity of the community and patrons.

Lloyd's Restaurant, 20 State St., Lowville, N. Y.

Lloyd's of Lowville, seen in this 1950s photograph, was owned and operated by Lloyd and Sophie Rassmussen. It was a restaurant previous to their ownership and is currently called Mr. Subs, a restaurant and takeout owned by Lila Tabolt. Lloyd's later moved to its current location on the small triangle between Utica Boulevard and Route 26.

Rossdale Farms built a dairy bar in 1954 across from Doviak Chevrolet, and the following year, an addition was built for use in pasteurizing and bottling milk for their route and currently the Lighthouse Restaurant. The Chevrolet dealership is now called Essenlohr's, and just beyond is the Schantz Building, which sold Studebaker automobiles and International Harvester products. There was also a Packard automobile agency in the same area built by Lloyd Loucks.

David S. Roberts was plant manager of the Sheffield, Slawson, and Decker Company, which later became Sheffield Farms Company in Malone. He later served in the same capacity at Freesbury and Vergennes in Vermont and was later promoted to dairy inspector and district superintendent. He moved to Lowville in 1917 and later served on the village board, was elected to two terms as mayor, and served seven terms as a trustee. When his workload increased with Sheffield Farms, he retired from politics. In 1941, he was in charge of construction for the company and traveled throughout New York State to all the milk plants, retiring after 39 years with the company. He passed away in 1963 at the age of 78. (Patricia Burke collection.)

The Lowville Milk and Cream Company was built in 1900 by Brayton B. Miller and his son Leon S. Miller. The name became Miller Richardson Cheese Company when Rufus J. Richardson was taken on as a partner. The name changed to Lowville Cold Storage Corporation when it became a subsidiary of the Kraft Phenix Cheese Company in 1928 and Kraft Cheese Company in 1940. A new plant was built and completed in 1971, and the old building was closed in 1972. The name became Kraft General Foods in 1995 and then Kraft Foods. (Below, Kraft Foods Collection.)

# *Three*

# RAILWAYS AND DEPOTS

The first excursion train of the Lowville and Beaver River Railroad left on January 13, 1906, and two days later, the first paying passengers departed. Special commuter tickets were sold to students from outlying areas who attended Lowville Academy. These firemen are waiting to greet incoming fire companies to bring them to the Independence Day parade location in 1909. (Carol Moshier collection.)

The New R.R. Depot
Lowville, N.Y.

During the next few years, mergers consolidated the Rome, Watertown and Ogdensburg Railroad. The Black River and Utica became the Utica and Black River Railroad. In 1891, New York Central and Hudson River Railroad leased the lines for 99 years, giving it ready-made access to the Thousand Islands, a persistent dream of Gilbert A. Blackmon.

N.Y.C.&H.R.R.R.
BRIDGE
AT
LOWVILLE, N.Y.

A 1907 photograph shows a train crossing the trestle on Water Street in Lowville loaded with lumber, logs, dairy, paper, and milk products heading south on the New York Central and Hudson River Railroad. A new 35-foot iron bridge was installed in 1910 to accommodate heavier traffic, especially during the Thousand Island season and transport of troops to Pine Plains.

Rail yards and buildings looking north before Trinity Avenue are shown in this 1907 photograph, with the Haberer Furniture Company and highly recognizable twin smokestacks and water tower at right. The front of the factory property is piled with culled logs.

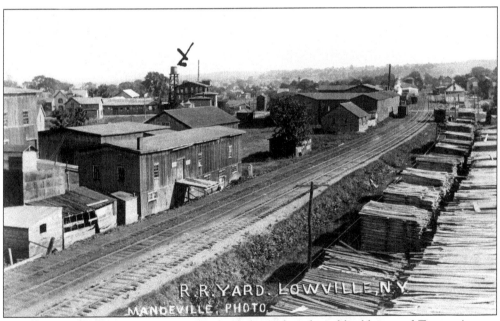

Looking south in this 1908 view are lumber-laden rail yards and buildings and Trinity Avenue with the Haberer Furniture Company, water tower, and smokestack (left). To the right and in front of the factory is the refinishing section directly across the street. It is now the location of Rings used car lot. The house on West Street and Trinity Avenue is still there.

An early-1900s photograph by William Mandeville shows (from left to right) Edward E. Williams with William L. Fellows, Glenn Smith, Frank Burk, Walt Stoddard, and an unidentified person with a shipment of calves at the rail yard to be loaded on the train. Williams, who regularly ran advertisements to buy stock, paid top prices for calves, hogs, and cattle and stands near the loaded car at the Lowville rail yards. The train was heading south with engine No. 1681, one of the workhorses used frequently by the line.

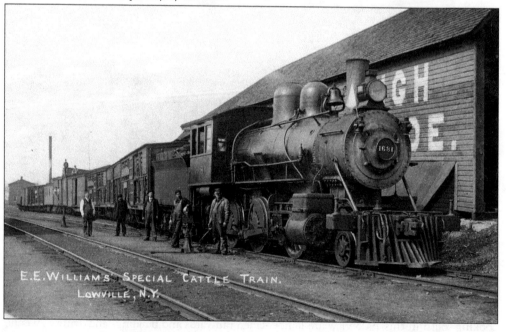

By the early 1900s, two short lines, the Lowville and Beaver River Railroad, northwest, and the Glenfield and Western Railroad, southwest, connected with the Utica-to-Ogdensburg main line of the New York Central Railroad at Lowville and Glenfield. Early tracks were often the site of derailments, as shown in this photograph taken between Martinsburg and Lowville. (Judy Adams collection.)

Lowville Station

The Lowville depot, with wagons awaiting the arrival of the train, is pictured near the W. C. Brown building at left. There are passengers sitting on the wagons and inside the depot as well.

This photograph of the Jackson Street depot, with unidentified men, shows the first shipment of legal beer that was received by rail in 1932 after Prohibition was repealed.

Unidentified men are loading a delivery truck with kegs of beer and preparing it for delivery to some of the local hotels and establishments that could once again legally serve the brew.

Engine No. 1923, 2-8-0, is shown here at the Lowville yards. It was a workhorse for the Lowville and Beaver River Railroad. (Carol Moshier collection.)

Rome, Watertown and Ogdensburg Railroad, advertising with New York Central and Black River Railroad Company, shows a timetable for the departure of trains from Lowville, both south and north, along with various advertisers from the area on the back.

## R. W. & O. RR. Time-Table.

*(N. Y. C. & H. R. RR. CO., Lessee.)*

| | |
|---|---|
| **BILLIARD PARLOR.** <br> A FINE LINE OF CIGARS, &C. <br> Shady Ave., Lowville, N. Y. <br> ALVIN McDONALD, Proprietor. | **O. P. C. G.** <br> GROCERIES AND PROVISIONS. <br> Come and see me. Cash——and you know the rest. <br> **ALDIS D. FOOT,** <br> ONE PRICE CASH GROCER, <br> 1 and 3 Dayan St., - Lowville, N. Y. |

**KELLOGG HOUSE.**
The only Centrally Located, First-Class Hotel in the City.
C. H. BATEMAN, Prop. - - - LOWVILLE, N. Y.

| | |
|---|---|
| **HEDDEN & MOORE,** <br> REAL ESTATE, FIRE, LIFE, <br> STEAM BOILER & ACCI- <br> DENT INSURANCE. <br> LOWVILLE, - - N. Y. | **E. J. ARTHUR,** <br> Dealer in <br> GROCERIES AND PROVISIONS, <br> Opposite Kellogg House, <br> LOWVILLE, - N. Y. |

**MILLER'S DYSPEPSIA CURE.**
A Sure Cure for Dyspepsia, Indigestion, Headache, Sour Stomach, and Heart Burn. Sold by All Druggists. R. L. Miller, manufacturer, Lowville, N. Y.

**BRUCE, THE WAGON MAN.**
Dealer in FINE CARRIAGES and TWO-HORSE WAGONS.
Call at BRUCE'S CARRIAGE EMPORIUM, Lowville, N. Y.

| Go to <br> **C. ELDRED'S** <br> For Candy made fresh every day, at wholesale and retail. 11 Shady Av, Lowville, N. Y. | **GILL HOUSE.** <br> A first-class House in every respect. Evening train stops 35 minutes for Supper. <br> Robert Gill, Manager, Carthage, N. Y. | **J. I. PUTNEY,** <br> Manufacturer of and Dealer in <br> DOMESTIC CIGARS. <br> Barber shop combined <br> 16 State St., <br> Carthage, - N. Y. |
|---|---|---|

THE CARTHAGE TRIBUNE IS THE BEST ADVERTISING MEDIUM IN NORTHERN N. Y.

The Lowville and Beaver River train returns to Lowville with a load of passengers from Croghan and New Bremen just south of the town garage on East Road near what is now the Nolt farm.

When the railroad was first planned, its biggest supporter was George A. Blackmon, who envisioned the track to run north from Lowville to East Road, across the "flats" to the Illingsworth Bridge, over the Black River, and toward New Bremen. Its length was 10½ miles. Passenger service was continued until January 10, 1947.

# Four

# FIRE DEPARTMENT

The Lowville Fire Department (built in 1870) was located on the north side of Dayan Street in back of the Smiley Building and made up of three departments, Alert Hook and Ladder Company No. 1, Active Hose Company, and Rescue Fire Company No. 2. In January 1980, the fire department moved to its present location on north State Street between the Baptist church and Key Bank.

*Active Hose Co. Lowville N. Y.*

Here are members of the Active Hose Company as they march in a parade heading south on State Street in front of the Kellogg building in the 1900s. This group of men cared for the hoses and carts in the organization. The first fire company was formed in 1829, with Stephen Leonard as captain. (Carol Moshier collection.)

When men of the Active Hose Company stood for this portrait in 1911, there were 56 members. There were 30 in their department, 26 in the hook and ladder company, and 4 torch boys, young men who carried torches for firemen at night and were learning the trade. (Carol Moshier collection.)

A parade inspection and review, with the police force, fire department, and village band, was an annual event. The Lowville Village Band and Fire Department are posed for this unusual photograph around 1907. All the names are unknown except for Charles A. Ryan of Ryans Candy. He served as the drum major for many years with the band and is in the third row in front of the tree.

The above photograph of firemen hosing down State Street in front of the Central Hotel was taken in the early 1900s. They may have been cleaning up after a recent fire by washing away debris, getting ready for a big parade, or cleaning up after the horses following a parade. (Gordon Allen collection.)

On May 30, 1889, smoke was discovered at the Dayan Street Opera House. Located just across the street, the fire department responded immediately. Once the fire extended to scenery, a strong southerly wind spread flames to William Morse's icehouse and house and Nicholas Boshart's house and barn on the corner of Cascade Avenue, west. Also lost in the inferno was the Merritt house, Samuel Bliss's blacksmith shop, and the Foot Block to the east. Firemen saved buildings on the opposite side of the street, including the fire department, by using the old hand pumper and emptying all the local wells and cisterns. Carthage firemen arrived to help save the Times, Conover, and Richardson Blocks, as well as the Baptist church on the north side of Dayan Street, but the George Wise property and the Lanpher Block were lost. By 3:00 a.m., the worst was over, and firemen continued to wet down the ruins. The image looks east from the destruction, with Lowville's 500-gallon LaFrance steam fire engine in the background. (Lowville Free Library Collection.)

The Moore building fire of February 1929 destroyed a two-story structure on the west side of State Street that was the location of the offices for Yale Moore Insurance, Roy Virkler, and Ryans Candy store on the ground floor. S. L. Meda constructed a modern brick building with offices and apartments overhead. At street level was Market Basket, a grocery store that stated the housewife's dollar would buy a lot more food there. (Gordon Allen collection.)

A 1930 photograph shows the aftermath of a fire in what is believed to be the stock barn of Glenn W. Smith on State Street south, which was near the yards of the Jackson Street depot. The fire killed two horses and four cows, along with 30 tons of hay, grain, and farm tools. Smith was wakened during the night after his wife noticed the fire and was able to remove the car from the burning building.

In 1954, fire roared through the Mammoth building, known locally as the A. N. Virkler Block, destroying O'Hara's Sport Shop, Kotary's Meat Market, and Farney Buick, which was filled with cars, parts, and equipment at the time. Firemen fought the blaze from a window in the G. A. Nortz Chrysler-Dodge business that was just 15 feet away, with only the side of the building being blistered. (Gordon Allen collection.)

A devastating fire broke out in the area above the Comfort Zone in October 1999 and managed to displace five businesses and dozens of residents that occupied the four historic brick buildings on the corner of State and Dayan Streets. A firewall at Western Auto prevented the blaze from spreading more. Nine surrounding fire companies came to assist Lowville Fire Department.

# Five

# HOUSES OF WORSHIP

This 1907 photograph shows the steeple of the Presbyterian church being painted. Organized in 1822, the church survived two disastrous fires, and in 1906, an addition of matching stone was built with an arch cut in the back wall of the church proper. The organ was moved to the new loft behind the pulpit, and new stained-glass windows and pews were installed. The front entrance was restored to its original form in 1937. (Carol Moshier collection.)

The Lowville Baptist Church was organized in 1824, but the formal building, shown in this 1908 photograph, was not constructed until 1890. The Reverend William W. Sawin served the church from 1940 to 1957, and during this time, extensive repairs were made in the basement and auditorium. Also improvements in equipment were made. The photograph below shows the interior altar, organ, and choir loft with decorative and intricate painting. Rev. Everett F. Reed is presently pastor.

A 1950 photograph of the choir loft and section in back of Reverend Sawin shows members, from left to right, (first row) Joyce Foote Pellam, Frances Gingerich, Henry Schaab, Jack Nortz, Bruce Virkler, Bessie Sawin (director), Sylvia Schaab Virkler (organist), Lawson Kilburn, Bruce Geer, Helen VanArnam, Carolyn Yousey Virkler, and Dorothy Myers; (second row) Bill Kilburn, Pete Nortz, Laura Buell, Joann Mowers, Bonnie Myers Colton, Marian Buhl, Vernon Gingerich, and Kennie Harris. (Carolyn Virkler collection.)

The John H. McCombe Tabernacle was erected in eight hours by 65 men in 1917 on the north corner of State Street and Waters Terrace for an ecumenical campaign that lasted several weeks. These tabernacles are usually of the simplest designs. The outside was covered with tar paper, the floor was covered with sawdust, and four large stoves kept the building warm. The building was 60 by 90 feet, seated 1,100 people, and required 25,000 feet of lumber to build. Irish evangelist McCombe was described as not a knocker but a booster. The interior photograph shows the benches made for the occasion, and in front is a large platform for the speaker and the choir.

St. Peter's Church was originally built in a pasture on the corner of Church Street and Highland Avenue in 1869. The above photograph dates from after 1898 when the tower and belfry were added to hang a bell that weighed one and a half tons, which was donated by John E. and George Haberer of Haberer Furniture. The church was later located on Shady Avenue in 1927 when it outgrew the first location. The cornerstone was laid on April 28, 1928, and the new church, shown in the photograph below, was dedicated on May 26, 1929. The beautiful stone edifice is a monument to the Reverend George L. Murray, pastor, and the parishioners who gave their support. A used Estey pipe organ was added in 1950. Fr. Timothy Soucy is the current pastor.

The first Methodist church services were held in 1798 at a schoolhouse. Land was purchased in 1823. The present church was later built at this location and dedicated in 1863. In 1915, under the leadership of Dr. Albert Loucks, an addition was built. During a terrible windstorm in 1929, the high spire with its golden dome was blown over, causing considerable damage to the roof, and the spire was lowered.

Services were held as early as 1800 in the home of Judge Nicholas Stowe for those in the Trinity Parish. In 1846, a lot was procured from J. W. Bostwick, and the cornerstone of the new church was laid. The building was removed to Shady Avenue and later became the rear part of the Arthur Feed Mill.

# Six

# Vintage Homes

Early sidewalks in Lowville were boardwalks, which made for a cleaner, drier surface to walk on, as seen in this 1907 photograph.

Horace Bush and Son sent this 1907 postcard to prospective clients advertising house paint. The card states it is the residence of Mrs. M. J. Leonard painted with Carter white lead and Spencer Kellogg's crystal boiled oil. The location is now occupied by North Country Estates Insurance. The brick building to the left is now Dunckel and King Attorneys. (Gordon Allen collection.)

Above is the Shady Avenue residence of Sidney S. Snell, who was a civil engineer for many years. The house is still in use as a private home.

The Franklin B. Hough home, seen here in 1910, is located on Collins Street. Hough, who was a physician, statistician, and naturalist of Lowville, wrote the *History of Lewis County* in 1860 and is well known for his forestry studies on preservation and renewal. The home remains in use today and is on the New York State historical register. (Michael K. Brown collection.)

James T. Galvin, who was a representative of the Mosler Safe Company for many years, lived in this home on Collins Street until he relocated to Waters Terrace. It is also the former home of the Dr. John Lormore family.

STANLEY MILLER RESIDENCE, LOWVILLE, N. Y.

The above photograph was taken around 1927 of the home that was built for Stanley B. Miller, who was a cheese tester for Kraft Foods and an automobile salesman. Miller was associated with Kraft Foods for 39 years until his retirement in 1953.

The above photograph shows the home of Charles L. Knapp as it appeared in 1915 during a summer lawn party. Knapp was a Republican U.S. senator from the 25th District and served from 1901 to 1911. Pictured at the table to the left are Grace Yousey, Grace Crane, and Mame. The view of the house from the rear shows a carriage pulling up to the porch with passengers ready to get out.

Reed's Terrace, Lowville, N.Y.

Bostwick Hall was originally the home of Isaac W. Bostwick, agent for Nicholas Low. It was built sometime around 1821 with limestone from the Talcottville quarry by artisans who constructed Constable Hall. At one time, the property included the entire area from the front of the 25-room home to State Street. It was formerly owned by the Reed family, and the street it is now located on, Reed's Terrace, was named for them. The second large home at left appears in the lower photograph and was owned by W. P. Rogers with an easterly view of Trinity Avenue. Bostwick Hall is now Bostwick Hall Massage Therapy, and the brick home in the second view is now Open Sky Healing Arts Center. (Above, Gordon Allen collection.)

Trinity Ave. South Side, Lowville, N. Y.

Photographs from 1914 show Dayan Street just below Easton Street at the sharp curve. The Cummings and Boissy brick homes are viewed on the north side, and the Herman house can be seen in both views and is located at the curve on the south side. (Above, Carolyn Virkler collection.)

The above photograph from 1911 shows the fountain and garden area for the DeWitt C. West estate on the corner of Clinton and State Streets. The property had a rambling ivy-covered stone wall that spanned the entire length from State to Easton Streets. The white house on the north side of Clinton Street is the former Cecil Waterman home.

The residence of Frank E. Brahmer on Park Avenue is shown in this 1912 photograph. Brahmer had a large clothing store on State Street south near the corner that now houses Jreck Subs. This residence was also the former home of Dr. Henry Geidel, D.D.S. (Gordon Allen collection.)

A 1911 photograph shows the house of William A. Miller, located on Trinity Avenue near Forest Avenue. A 50th wedding anniversary was held here for his wife's parents, Elon and Viola Dodge of Turin, on December 10, 1910.

An early-1900s photograph of Park Avenue looking north near Trinity Avenue shows the Edwin J. Arthur (left) and Cleveland D. Manville homes.

The A. Hauver home on the west side of Easton Street is shown in this 1911 photograph looking north on Clinton Street. The large stone wall (right) is part of the DeWitt C. West estate on State Street. A view of the building's cupola is shown at right, and it was the former Benchmark Family Service child care center on State Street.

This early-1900s view shows the home of blacksmith Noah Yousey on the north side of Stow Street at the lower end where his son Earl was born and raised.

RESIDENCE of B.J.HATMAKER. LOWVILLE, N.Y.

The B. J. Hatmaker residence and Civil War monument on State Street west are seen in the above 1911 photograph and appear much the same today. The residence was formerly the Health Culture Home, a sanitarium owned by Dr. E. H. Bush. It closed in 1908. It is currently the location of the Victoria Guest House.

RESIDENCE OF A.G.GASSER. Lowville.N.Y. Aug. 15, 1908.

Shown in this 1908 photograph is the home of Alpheus G. Gasser. Gasser traveled heavily as a salesman for the Mosler Safe and Lock Company.

Looking west toward State Street in this 1906 photograph, Elm Street, the location of the Ira Sharp home, is shown. Sharp served as supervisor of Lowville for five years, was a breeder of Cheshire swine, was a hop and hay grower, and owned a 500-tree maple sugar orchard. The photograph below shows the living room at the Sharp home. (Michael K. Brown collection.)

This view is looking north on Park Avenue, formerly called Leonard Street, in the early 1900s. Most of the property on the west side of the street was owned by the John Doig family, and the house on the left is the former home of George W. Fowler.

A 1911 view of the north side of Shady Avenue shows the Hyram Gowdy house that was later purchased in 1926 by St. Peter's parish for the construction of a new church. The house on the corner in the background now serves as the parish offices.

This late-1890s photograph looks east and shows Trinity Avenue at State Street with Trinity Church and the parsonage on the north side. The fencing, shown to the south, is part of Bostwick Hall, owned by T. Miller Reed at the time, whose property extended to State Street. Reed, a lawyer, served as district attorney for nine years. The estate was later owned by his son George S. Reed.

An 1890s view of Highland Avenue, which runs into Church Street, shows the neighborhood when St. Peter's Church was located on the corner. Looking east, the home of James O'Connor can be seen on the north side, and one of the homes on the south side was owned by Patrick and Bridget Dunn.

A 1918 view of Shady Avenue at the Park Avenue intersection shows some of the homes that still exist today. The photograph was taken looking southwest toward State Street, and the house at far left is now painted in period colors of raspberry with a cream and turquoise trim. Looking west toward the trees, the home described below can be seen just at their edge.

This was the home of John G. Moshier on the south side of Shady Avenue as seen in the 1890s. Moshier was an early tanner and a retired farmer with 240 acres in West Martinsburg, including 5 acres of hops, 40 cows, and 10 head of young cattle. The home is still occupied and is directly across from St. Peter's Church. (Michael K. Brown collection.)

This 1909 photograph of Clinton Street was taken looking east just below Easton Street and shows the fence of the large estate of DeWitt C. West. The property was bounded from Easton to State Streets and enclosed by a stone fence. Most recently, Benchmark Family Service occupied the building on this corner lot on State Street.

A bird's-eye view of the village, taken in 1909, shows the valley with the Black River overflowing its banks. At the time, Lowville had quite the mixture of estates, modest homes, and farms. The large building and barn in the center are the Lewis County Home and grounds.

# *Seven*

# BANDS AND PARADES

Clinton Alexander and his daughter are
pictured in this early-1900s photograph
by William Mandeville titled "Tootie in a
Tooter." Alexander and his wife, Madeline,
lived on State Street, and he played in
the village band for many years. (Gordon
Allen collection.)

The village band has always been a presence, in one form or another. Dr. Franklin B. Hough's *A History of Lewis County* mentions the existence of a Union band in 1826 and a saxhorn band in the fall of 1857. In the following images from 1908 and 1909, one person stands out in presence and uniform, Charles H. Ryan of Ryans Candy store. He led the band in every parade for years as a drum major and is seen in the top row (above) and the far right (below). Clinton Alexander, who appeared on the first page of this chapter with his tuba, can also be seen in the image below standing in back of Ryan.

The Zenith Chapter, No. 346, Order of the Eastern Star, met on Flag Day, June 20, 1912, in its meeting rooms next to the Masonic temple. The initiatory degree was conferred following a large banquet for more than 100 persons who attended the gathering. The chapter's first matron was Sr. Emma Mooney, and Alonzo S. Dano the first patron.

In this photograph, dated August 27, 1913, two bands are seen marching north on State Street during the Lewis County Fair and Boosters Carnival, which featured a firemen's parade with elaborate decorations of flags and buntings on the Bank of Lowville building and other businesses.

The Lowville Band is shown in this image entering State Street from Dayan Street with Charles H. Ryan checking its progress in front.

The Memorial Day parade of 1914 was a grand production by the entire community that honored the ranks of the old veterans of the Civil War. In attendance were 400 schoolchildren in white uniforms, who were directed by principal William F. Breeze. Children were grouped in eight grades and led by their teachers, and a program was held at the soldiers' and sailors' monument where they sang patriotic songs. Decorated automobiles brought the veterans to the two cemeteries where graves of fallen comrades were decorated with flowers.

Another image of Memorial Day in 1914 was taken by photographer George Carter near the soldiers' and sailors' monument with the homes of Charles Lewis and Charles E. Douglass, M.D., in the background. Schoolchildren can be seen marching around the monument with fire department members to the left of the statue.

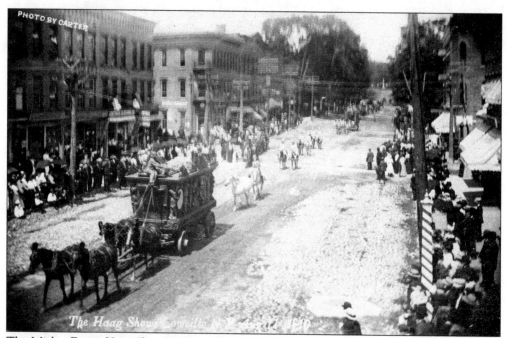

The *Mighty Ernest Haag Show* was a traveling circus that came to Lowville in 1910. The huge, heavily carved Columbus-John Smith bandwagon led the parade on State Street and was followed by another wagon that featured a steam calliope and player Nellie King Oram. (Judy Adams collection.)

94

This photograph of the village band marching south on State Street is believed to have been taken in 1908 during an annual review parade that the fire department conducted every spring. Charles H. Ryan is leading the group.

The Lowville Band is shown in front of the Times Building marching in the 1913 Lowville Fair and Boosters Carnival parade. The photograph was taken by Carter.

These two 1913 photographs, one taken during the day and the other after dark, show the Doig Block and Kellogg House while they were decorated for the Lewis County Fair and Boosters Carnival. Business owners and tenants paid up to $1,000 for the elaborate buntings viewed on the front of the buildings that were decorated by M. J. Crandall and his crew of assistants from Fulton and took almost a week of preparation and two carloads of material. The Wetmore Electric Company was in charge of lighting, and several thousand bulbs spanned the streets in rope form with many artistic designs. Buildings were illuminated from Campbell Street to the monument at the end of State Street.

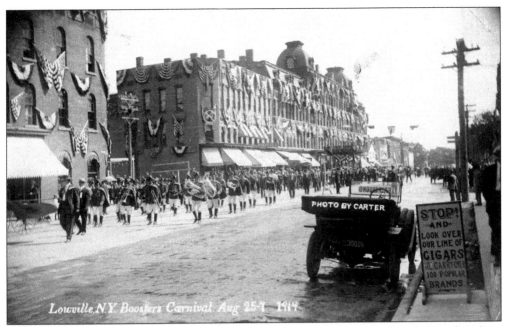

This 1914 George Carter photograph from in front of the Bank of Lowville is believed to show the Oldfield Military Band of Boonville at the booster parade in August marching north on State Street. The parade was made up of seven divisions and presented the "Story of Uncle Sam" as the theme.

Pictured on June 12, 1908, the U.S. Cavalry and wagons are seen at the Mill Creek bridge on State Street on their way to Pine Camp, which eventually became Fort Drum. Gen. Frederick Dent Grant, son of Pres. Ulysses S. Grant, held large summer maneuvers at Pine Plains beginning that year.

Soldiers, pictured here in 1908, include U.S. Army regulars from throughout the northeastern United States and National Guardsmen from New York, Massachusetts, Pennsylvania, and New Jersey. Nearly 16,000 soldiers poured into tent encampments north of the Black River near Watertown and proved to be a success with the location formally selected by the U.S. Army as a permanent training area. In 1909, Pine Camp Military Reservation was established, and beginning in 1910, the army purchased land and began constructing buildings at Pine Camp. In 1941, Pine Camp was selected as a divisional training facility with a division cantonment constructed. The area expanded to 110,000 acres with numerous farms and homesteads purchased, and families moved to new locations. Five villages, including Sterlingville, vanished from the map after this last growth spurt.

10ᵗʰ Cavalry at Lowville N.Y. July 29ᵗʰ 1910.

On July 28, 1910, a notice in the *Lowville Journal and Republican* appeared, announcing that the 10th Regiment, black veterans of San Juan Hill, would pass through Lowville on the following day. The regiment marched to Pine Plains from Fort Ethan Allen in Vermont, a distance of 280 miles, with about 700 men and 800 horses. They were due to arrive in Lowville around 9:00 a.m., and because of construction on Route 26, they were detoured to the C. Blon Arthur farm road and down Stow Street through the village. At the State Street bridge, the cavalry was met by the Lowville Band and other local dignitaries from the community and from service groups. All citizens were invited to join the reception for the group along the parade route, and businesses and homes were requested to display the flag. The cavalry had its own 30-piece mounted band, and during the reception hour, a concert program was presented by them. According to official records, the 10th Regiment made Theodore Roosevelt's Rough Riders charge at San Juan Hill the success it was by coming to the rescue when troops were beginning to weaken.

The Grand Army of the Republic (GAR), photographed here in 1908, marched onto Valley Street (now Rural Avenue) from Cascade Avenue to visit veterans' graves at the Lowville Rural Cemetery on Memorial Day. The following is an excerpt from "The Little Green Tents," a poem by Walt Mason: "And the brave men left, so old, so few, were young and stalwart in sixty-two, when they went to war away." (Carol Moshier collection.)

On June 5, 1913, George Carter photographed the funeral procession for Dr. Frederick A. Crane. Shown is a group from one of the fraternal organizations of which he was a member, as they marched north on State Street. He served as president of the village for two years, and for more than 30 years, he was house physician at the county home. Crane was educated at Whitesboro Seminary and studied under his uncle Dr. Deloss Crane at Holland Patent. All businesses were closed for this solemn occasion.

# *Eight*

# LEWIS COUNTY FAIR

Fairgoers stroll the grounds as they check on new farm equipment, grab a bite to eat, or enjoy the amusement rides in back of the grandstand at the Lewis County Fair on August 28, 1913.

Lowville N.Y.

Lowville village band members are entering Forest Park at the archway of the Dewitt Street entrance while others cross the track in front of the grandstand from the infield in these 1907 photographs. Bands attending the parade usually performed in concert at various times during the week, and exhibits under the bandstand included floral arrangements, needlework, and painted china. (Above, Carol Moshier collection.)

why don't you write

Maude

New York governor Charles E. Hughes (right) is pictured as he prepared to join the parade for the Lewis County Fair on August 28, 1907. The governor arrived by special train for the event and delivered an eloquent speech for the occasion. Hughes, who was in office from 1907 to 1910, also attended the Oneida County Fair in Boonville. (Carol Moshier collection.)

For the booster carnival parade, cars were gaily decorated with special themes during fair week. The car of L. Charles Davenport, in a before image, took second place in 1913 with decorations that were rented from Mr. Crandall, just north of the Methodist parsonage. A total of 108 decorated cars entered the two-mile-long event, vying for top honors. (Gordon Allen collection.)

A family in a horse-drawn fringed surrey is seen in this 1896 photograph getting ready to go to the Lewis County Fair. The event was usually an all-day affair that began early in the morning and lasted until late in the afternoon. Special events were also scheduled at the town hall for the evening hours.

This 1888 Pearline Soap trade card shows a list of prizes awarded at the fair for that year on the reverse. An 18-pound box of laundry soap was presented for the best varieties of apples, best jar of butter, best patchwork quilt, and jars of fruit.

A Percheron stallion, owned by C. L. Yousey and Peter S. Noftsier of Croghan, was photographed in Lowville on Dayan Street in the early 1900s. Draft horses were at a premium at this time, and pulls were a special event at every local fair for many years. Many were registered in the *American Stud Book*, with each carrying a separate number. (Gordon Allen collection.)

This "Rapid Transit"—a pony cart pulled by two yoked pigs—appeared at the 1909 Lewis County Agricultural Fair and seemed to draw a good bit of attention at Forest Park. (Gordon Allen collection.)

Farm equipment was always popular at the fair, as shown at the tent of the Superior Drill Company (left), which manufactured corn-planting drills, hollow spikes that drilled into the ground and deposited a seed. Another popular destination was the Ferris wheel, which took the rider up to the top of the trees for a better look around the fairgrounds. These photographs were taken in back of the grandstand at the 1909 fair. The ride never seemed to be vacant in these pictures.

Shuttle buses brought visitors to the Lewis County Fair and exposition at Forest Park from the front of Kellogg House in 1909. Featured as an old home week, there were many great attractions offered, including low excursion rates on the railroads, music by the Lowville and Boonville bands, and baseball games that were always a favorite.

Strolling on the Bostwick Street side of the fairgrounds, fairgoers had much to choose from for entertainment on August 28, 1913. The Lowville and Port Leyden bands offered concerts, and draft horse pulls and DeRenzo and Ladue acrobats were also featured.

"STEEPLECHASE," LEWIS CO. FAIR, LOWVILLE, N.Y.                    MANDEVILLE PHOTO.

Horse racing has been a popular event at the Lewis County Fair since before the early 1900s. Pictured are the steeplechase at the grandstand in 1906 (above) and horses rounding the first turn of the track in 1908 (below). Both photographs were taken by William Mandeville.

LEWIS CO. FAIR, LOWVILLE, N.Y.                    MANDEVILLE PHOTO.

A very popular event in the booster carnival and parade was decorating cars. Car tops were suggested to be down and loaded with as many decorations as possible. All were to meet at the monument park on State Street and then travel to Campbell Street, Dayan Street, Shady Avenue, Park Avenue, Bostwick Street, then back to State Street and to the Bateman where prizes were awarded. Leon S. Miller won first prize in 1913, as shown in the above photograph by William Mandeville. In 1914, Rufus J. Richardson's gaily decorated Pierce-Arrow took two first-place prizes from both the carnival and the agricultural society. (Above, Gordon Allen collection.)

Second prize in the 1914 automobile parade went to Leon S. Miller, as shown in this William Mandeville photograph, for his nautical theme. Although Charles Pelton's car did not receive any awards, it still warranted having a photograph taken to honor the occasion. First prize received $50 from the agricultural society.

Baseball games were very popular events, as seen in this 1906 photograph taken of the infield area of the fairgrounds track. Premiums were awarded to the winners of the events often between Lowville, Carthage, Boonville, Port Leyden, Trenton, Harrisville, Lyons Falls, and Old Forge-Fulton Chain.

Buggies line up around the track for the final day in this photograph of the 1912 fair, which included the grand parade of premium stock, an auction sale of registered stock in front of the grandstand, and the airplane flight by Capt. Thomas S. Baldwin.

Photo By Carter

BALDWIN RED DEVIL BI-PLANE.

Lowville NY Lewis Co Fair week Aug 28-1913.

This George Carter photograph shows Capt. Thomas S. Baldwin and his Red Devil biplane as they appeared at the Lewis County Fair on August 28, 1913. By 1911, Baldwin had built several airplanes and had gained extensive experience as a stunt pilot and exhibitionist. He began testing a new airplane in the spring of 1911 similar to the basic Curtiss pusher design but different in that it was constructed of steel tubing. It was powered by a 60-horsepower Hall-Scott V-8 engine, and Baldwin called his new machine the Red Devil. Baldwin built approximately six Red Devils, and most were powered by the Hall-Scott engine, but Curtiss engines were also occasionally used. Baldwin's appearance at the fair was an extremely popular event that drew tremendous crowds.

# *Nine*

# ACADEMY AND SCHOOLS

The third such building in its history, Lowville Academy is shown in this 1922 photograph, just two years before a very difficult decision was made to tear down its hallowed walls and start anew.

Students pose on the lattice veranda of Lowville Academy in this 1908 William Mandeville image (above) that was taken at the end of the school year. Construction began on this academy in 1836 when a previous structure, built on the same location, failed after only 10 short years. The photograph below was taken when the institution was a centenarian. This academy was to last until 1924 when its bricks were torn down once again to begin the next chapter in its history. (Above, Carol Moshier collection.)

Lowville State Street School, with its students and teachers, is shown in this 1908 Mandeville photograph. The school, now a private residence, was sold in 1926 along with the Jackson Street School and East State Street School, also known as Seven Day Settlement School, when the new Lowville Academy was completed.

"A building of mellowing charm and grace / Reflecting the best of its time and race, Again for its students a meeting place / our own Academy." "The River of Time," a poem written by Alice E. Allen, was read by her at the 125th anniversary banquet on June 26, 1933, at the newly completed academy.

A 1912 varsity baseball team from Lowville Academy is pictured. From left to right are (first row) ? Brown, Elmer Kieb, and ? Claffey; (second row) Byron Bowen, Anson Kieb, Prof. William F. Breeze, ? Johnson, and ? O'Neil; (third row) Walter McGrath, ? Benedict, W. Breen, ? Phelps, ? Bradey, and Miller Moran.

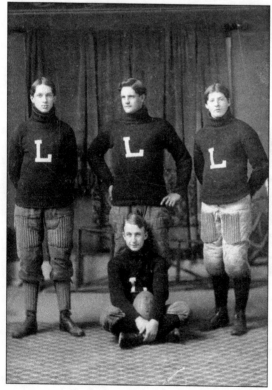

Pictured is the 1902 backfield of the Lowville Academy varsity football team that helped win the northern New York championship. From left to right are Brown Ralston, right halfback; Leroy Doxtater, fullback; Jesse Cooke, left halfback; and (in front) James Goutremout, quarterback and captain. (Michael K. Brown collection.)

The 1931 Lowville Academy varsity football team is shown in this William Mandeville photograph. From left to right are (first row) C. Bush, P. Thomas, J. Russum, and Phillip Klett; (second row) Tony Paczkowski, George Repave, Phillip Payne, Russell Duflo (captain), Beryl Moran, Robert Lameureaux, and Loren Bush; (third row) Verle Walters, D. Ramage, John Bush, Jack Russum, Roger Trombly, H. Humphrey, F. Walters, L. Meda, and coach Walter O'Connell. Scores of games for the season included Lowville 0, Tupper Lake 6; Lowville 7, St. Aloysius 0; Lowville 0, Herkimer 58; Lowville 0, Canastota 6; Lowville 7, Phoenix 0; and Lowville 14, Pulaski 0.

A photograph taken by George Carter in 1913 shows younger school-aged children dressed in white naval uniforms for the Memorial Day parade. Many are carrying American flags.

This first-grade class at Lowville had its photograph taken outside in 1940. From left to right are (first row) Joe Easton, Louis Bush, Wilfred Campany, Art Farney, unidentified, ? Coffin, Joyce Foote, Joyce Loson, and Lewis Moselle; (second row) James O'Connell, Louis Skaddock, Rita Joy, Nancy Garnham, Mary Jane Jones, Elmer Roggie, Sue Finn, Anna Jean Kloster, and Pete Nortz; (third row) unidentified, ? Putnam, Mary Lou Bach, Gregory Boshart, Bill VerSchneider, Mary Schantz, unidentified, Barb Duflo, David Spencer, Jean Hulbert, Wanda Veitch, and Gerald Boshart. (Gordon Allen collection.)

# *Ten*

# MISCELLANEOUS SPECIAL EVENTS

CARTER PHOTO                    N.Y. City Salvation Army Band Lowville N.Y. April 20ᵗʰ 1917.

An open-air concert was given by the Salvation Army Band from New York City in front of Brahmer's on April 20, 1917, as seen in this Carter photograph. The band of 35 musicians and singers was en route to Ogdensburg to participate in the dedication of the new Salvation Army building there.

SOLDIER'S MONUMENT.
LOWVILLE, N.Y. MANDEVILLE, PHOTO.

Erected on a small park in front of the Presbyterian church on North State Street, the GAR monument bears the names of 267 men who were killed or later died from injuries received at the battles of Bull Run, Cold Harbor, Gettysburg, Chattanooga, Antietam, Petersburg, Seven Pines, and Wilderness and the prison at Andersonville. Recently placed on the New York State Register of Historic Places, it was manufactured by Monumental Bronze Company of Bridgeport, Connecticut. Joseph Dieffendorf, who enlisted at the age of 38 in 1861, is one of the names listed on the statue base. He served as a private with the 97th New York Volunteers and was one of a handful of black soldiers who served in white companies nearly two years before Pres. Abraham Lincoln formally authorized the use of troops of African descent. Approximately 2,500 volunteers served from Lewis County. Save our Statue is a nonprofit group that has worked tirelessly to have the statue restored and hopes to have enough funds soon to start the process.

The 50th anniversary reunion of the 3rd Battalion Black River Artillery of the Fifth New York Heavy Artillery was held on August 20, 1912, in Lowville. Lewis County raised four companies for the war, and the 600 men were sent to Sackets Harbor and on to Washington, D.C. V. Lansing Waters was president of the GAR Association.

These 74 men of the 4th Contingent from Lewis County pose for a William Mandeville portrait just before their departure to Camp Devens, Massachusetts, on February 23, 1918. At a dinner given in their honor the night before at the Club House, the men were wished Godspeed by the Home Defense Committee. The former Paul Abbott home, built in 1812, appears in the background.

On February 1, 1918, Allen McMullen, with his team of six Great Danes, embarked on his journey to New York City where the dog team was turned over to the Red Cross. McMullen had trained these dogs, one as large as 35 inches tall, to be used on the western front battle line to bring ammunition and supplies to the troops.

These people are pictured at the Gallup hunting party in 1928. From left to right are Frank Miller of Buffalo, Jerome Jeffrey of Buffalo, Harold "Peb" Peebles of Lowville, Babe ? of Connecticut, Cal Chapin of Buffalo, Ed Kohler of Rochester, unidentified of Connecticut, Walter Kohler of Lowville, Bill Taylor of Rochester, Harvey Gallup of Lowville, and Howard Kohler of Buffalo. The photograph was taken by Judson Gallup. (Bonnie Virkler collection.)

As shown in the 1907 photograph above, Mill Creek was a popular spot during the summer both for swimming in the hole farther up the stream and for picturesque views near East State Street. A winter view (right) of the ravine at Morrison's Falls at Mill Creek near the State Street bridge in 1908 shows the dam that was replaced in the summer of 1909. The old dam was built in 1854 by Jeremiah Mott, owner of the Morrison Grist Mill. Dynamite was attempted twice, with the first charge unsuccessful. The second attempt sprayed stones 200 feet in the air, damaging Nortz's Bottling Works roof. Work was completed by hand thereafter. The building on the right is currently Sno-Belt Housing, and at left is the former Papa Joe's.

Winter travel was a challenge at the bad curve on Dayan Street, even in 1908, with the only means of transportation being the horse and cutter on the snow-covered streets. The view below shows another cutter in front of John Quinn's Harness Shop. The three buildings below are now where the Commons is located.

Thomas B. Fowler sent this photograph to a family member stating he had shoveled enough snow to dig a canal from Lowville to Rome in 1916. The view is in front of the Fowler and Sons store on the west side of State Street. While across State Street, other downtown businesses suffered the same fate, and yet all survived hardships of those times. Anne Bradstreet stated, "If we had no winter, the spring would not be so pleasant."

Every fall, the Lowville Business Association settles down after a busy summer season and manages yet another celebration with the Cream Cheese Festival to celebrate Kraft Foods, the world's largest cream cheese manufacturing plant in the world. Daylong activities include live music, food, local artists, family-oriented games, and a discovery park and petting zoo for the children. Kraft employees make and serve a cheesecake that measures 8 feet by 25 feet—some of the largest cheesecakes ever made. The fifth-annual Cream Cheese Festival is scheduled for Saturday, September 19, 2009.

# ABOUT THE SOCIETIES

Constable Hall Association and the Lewis County Historical Society are dedicated to the collection and preservation of local history. Both organizations have a formidable collection of artifacts that illustrate the tenacity of north country residents from the 1790s to the present century.

Constable Hall Association began in 1949 when John Constable sold his family home to Mr. and Mrs. Harry Lewis and his sister Grace Cornwall. Constable Hall is listed on the National Register of Historic Places as a historic home museum. In 1791, William Constable Sr. bought 3.8 million acres (10 percent of New York State). Eventually this real estate was divided into five counties and portions of several others. William Constable Jr. and his wife, Mary Eliza, built the hall between 1810 and 1819. Five generations of the family lived in this Georgian country manor. From the end of May to mid-October, guided tours are provided for visitors. Call 315-397-2323 for specific summer hours. The Constable Hall is located at 5909 John Street, Constableville, NY 13325.

Since 1927, the Lewis County Historical Society has been preserving the history of Lewis County. According to its charter, the society's purpose is to preserve items and documents of historic significance to Lewis County. The facility uses a Masonic lodge room for exhibits in the summer. During the winter, the room is used for the Black River Valley Concert series. Research facilities for local history and genealogy are available during the summer season. The society's latest project is the restoration of the Walter Martin mansion in Martinsburg. Call 315-376-8957 for specific hours. The society is located at 7553 South State Street, Lowville, NY 13367.

Visit us at
arcadiapublishing.com

Printed in the USA
CPSIA information can be obtained
at www.ICGtesting.com
LVHW071459041223
765647LV00008B/146

9 781531 642594